A SAFE *and* HAPPY PLACE

A DAUGHTER'S REFLECTIONS

SARA HOFFMAN MOCKETT

LUMINARE PRESS

WWW.LUMINAREPRESS.COM

A Safe and Happy Place: A Daughter's Reflections
© 2015 Sara Hoffman Mockett

Printed in the United States of America

Cover Design: Claire Last

Luminare Press
467 W 17th Ave
Eugene, OR 97401
www.luminarepress.com

LCCN: 2015953888
ISBN: 978-1-937303-63-1

Contents

FLORENCE

I never met my maternal grandmother, Florence Ingersoll. Some of the stories of her life were handed down to me by my mother, Alice, her daughter. My mother never remembered a time when her mother, Florence, was not ill.

FLORENCE'S SURGERY WAS SCHEDULED FOR MONDAY morning at 9 am on May 15, 1925. She feared doctors and hospitals, but the removal of her spleen held new hope for ending her long struggle with the vapors, which had stolen all joy in her life, and depleted her energy for far too long. Depression first descended upon Florence seventeen years ago in 1907, after the birth of her second daughter.

Her doctor had explained to her that the source of her feelings of hopelessness and listlessness was in the hypochondria, that portion of the abdomen that was the seat of the emotions. It contained the liver, gallbladder and the spleen. The removal of the spleen would be a cure for her depression and promised a return to happiness and joy.

Some days were better than others for Florence,

but she spent most of her time in her room with little strength to do more than address the daily decisions required in running the household – decisions that only she could make. There were meals to be planned, clothing to be selected for the girls from the possible choices purchased by the maid, correspondence to be answered, and household help to supervise. Her husband, Robert, spent long days at the office. He had recently been appointed secretary of the Milton Bradley Company in Springfield, Massachusetts, a position he took on in 1908 while his father-in-law, the founder, was still alive. Robert was to serve as secretary of the Company for thirty-three years, and briefly as President at the end of his career in 1941. His unfailing qualities of loyalty, and devotion to detail characterized Robert Ingersoll's work throughout his long years with the Company

In addition to the immediate family, Robert and Florence Ingersoll's household consisted of the cook, the chauffeur, the upstairs maid and the downstairs maid. Mabel, the cook, and her husband, Tom, had been reliable employees for many years, and had become a part of the family. Florence had had to advertise more often than she would like, however, for the maids.

The maids were expected to tend to the usual housework: supervise the girls, shop for their clothing, and help with their homework, as well as wait on Florence. If Florence was sleeping, it was the maids' responsibility to be sure that the children were quiet and did not disturb their mother. This was a home where a great deal of the thought and concern centered around Florence and on her depression.

Even if Florence had had more strength and enthusiasm, the ways she could have directed it were limited. Women at this time did not work outside the home, or even envision themselves doing anything more than running their households and maintaining social connections. For women of the upper class, it was considered demeaning to engage in any household work, or even to run and play with their children.

ON THE MORNING OF HER SURGERY, FLORENCE WAS ANXious, as one might expect, but she was looking forward to the return of her cheerful, more energetic self. Robert had taken the day off from work to drive her to Chapin Memorial Hospital, and to be there when she came out of the recovery room. It was a clear day in mid May, and the air was soft and warm. They both admired the blaze of color – red, yellow, purple and blue in neighboring yards as they drove past in their Model T Ford. Robert enjoyed riding about the city in this amazing new invention, but Florence still missed the horse and carriage that they had had for most of their married life.

The doctor greeted them when they arrived at the hospital and reassured them that all should go well. Florence was whisked off to be prepared for surgery, and Robert settled down in the waiting room with a good book. The hospital staff suggested that he go home. They could call him when the surgery was over. He insisted that he stay, however. He wanted to be close by.

ROBERT INGERSOLL WAS BORN IN 1875 AND EDUCATED AT the State Military Institute of Florida. Upon the outbreak of the Spanish American War, he enlisted in the 2nd Infantry Regiment and served in the Santiago Campaign. Before going to Cuba, handsome, affable Bob had been a frequent visitor at the Bradley home at 515 State Street in Springfield, where he was soon recognized as Florence's favorite beau. He was a tall, kindly man, and those who knew him well were aware that it was impossible for him to act in any way but decently. Rarely was he seen without a tie or without his watch bob in his vest pocket.

During the war he wrote daily letters home from the front to his mother, his father, his grandfather and to Florence. His letters to his parents always mentioned Florence, and his wish that they look out for her. In a letter dated June 6, 1898, he wrote: "I've just written to Florence. Dear girl keep her with you all you can Mother. She loves you and you will be a comfort to each other." Robert Ingersoll and Florence Bradley were married October 10, 1899, soon after he returned from the war, and went to work for the Milton Bradley Company. The wedding was held at the house of her father. Florence was 25 years old. Their two daughters, Rachel and Alice, were born in 1902 and 1907 respectively.

Florence – Part 2

Robert tried to concentrate on the book he was reading, but his mind kept wandering to his dear wife, Florence, and what was happening in the operating room. As deeply as he cared for her, there was absolutely nothing he could do, but wait and pray. He had done a great deal of reading and research about splenectomies – the surgery that was thought to be a cure for hypochondria and for pernicious anemia. He had learned that there was some risk, as with any surgery, but that the mortality rate had dropped significantly in the past 20 years from 40% to less than 5%. The odds were certainly in favor of a positive outcome. The doctors had told him that there was no reason to be unduly concerned. Soon it would be over and Florence would regain her strength and joyful outlook.

Just when he thought he could wait no longer, the surgeon appeared to report that the surgery was over and that Florence was doing well. They would let him know when he could see her. Robert felt a blessed sense of relief flow through him, and a heightened awareness of the beautiful blue sky, the chirping birds, and the bright, warm sun outside the hospital window. Robert's relief was short-lived, however. A half hour later the ashen-faced doctor came to sadly report that Florence had suffered from a post operative hemorrhage and had died. She was 51 years old.

The bright, warm spring day of May 15, 1925, suddenly turned grey. Robert didn't notice the colorful spring flowers along the roadway as he drove home alone in his new Model T Ford. All he could think of was his dear Florence, and that he would never see her again. His thoughts soon turned to his two daughters and the devastating news that was now his task to share. Rachel, 23 years old, was living in Boston – he would call her this evening. Alice, 17 years old, usually arrived home from the nearby Central High School around 3:30 pm. He had a little time yet to prepare for his difficult task.

Outgoing, enthusiastic Alice burst breathless into the house at 3:20 pm. One look at her beloved father's face and she knew immediately that something was terribly, terribly wrong. She was not prepared, however, for the impossible truth that her mother was dead. "No, no," she cried out, and unexpectedly rushed away and locked herself in the front hall closet.

Alice was my mother. She told me this story many times through the years. She stayed in the closet for several hours trying to grapple with the life changing news she had just received. Mother could not remember a time when her mother, Florence, had been active and involved in life. She had always had a close relationship with her mother, however, and she loved her deeply. The loss was profound, and would affect the rest of her life.

Personally, I have always wondered whether my grand-mother's depression might not have been, at least partially, the result of being a capable woman living in an era when women in her social setting had limited outlets for their talents and intellectual gifts. They could plan meals, but they could not cook. They could run a household, but they could not clean. They could have children, but they did not have to care for them all the time, they could own a car, but they could not drive. In many ways, they were prisoners in their own homes. They were prisoners of their social class.

ALICE

M Y MOTHER, ALICE BRADLEY INGERSOLL, WAS BORN in 1907 in Springfield, Massachusetts. At that time, the family was living in a double house at 517 State Street. Her maternal grandparents, Milton and Ellen Bradley, lived in one half, and the Ingersoll family occupied the other. Each half was a full two stories. Connecting the two houses was an inner door that was always kept unlocked. Cheerful, round faced, little Alice was free to go back and forth between the two houses whenever she wanted to visit her grandparents. Outside, in front of the house, there was the steady excitement of colorful trolley cars traveling back and forth down the middle of the street.

When Alice was seven the family moved from State Street to 79 Bowdoin Street, a larger three-story Victorian house just a few blocks away. It was here that her parents hired extra help – a cook, a second girl and a chauffer. Young Alice was busy and curious. She not only wanted to know what the cook was doing in the kitchen, she wanted to help. The cook, however, could not be bothered with a child under foot, and shooed her away. The second girl, who waited on table and took care of the dining room, took an interest in Alice, however, and was more receptive to her eagerness to learn. She allowed Alice to help polish the silver, to help set the table, and she thoughtfully answered the child's unending questions.

There was also a sewing lady who came to the house once a week, and Alice was especially fascinated by watching her hands fly over the fabric, and by the magical spin of the wheel on the treadle sewing machine. Whenever she had a little extra time, the sewing lady would let Alice sit at the sewing machine and practice trying to make stitches in a straight line.

In spite of her limited energy, Florence, who had taken to her bed when she was 33 years old, shortly after Alice was born, was a caring, involved mother. Alice learned many things from her mother. Florence taught young Alice to carefully roll up the fabric scraps after the sewing lady left, and store them neatly in a drawer. She also taught Alice to shop by introducing her to the sales people she knew in town. When she got older, Alice was allowed to go downtown alone on the trolley to pick out two dresses that she liked with the help of the sales person her mother knew. She would then bring the dresses home, and Florence would select the one to keep.

Later, when Florence became even more frail, a companion was hired to assist her and to keep her company. Her name was also Florence, which certainly must have created a bit of confusion from time to time. Several women had applied for the position, but Robert was particularly impressed by Miss Jennings' outgoing, personable manner. She was also quite attractive and stylish, so certainly must have offered some positive life to the Ingersoll home in many ways. Florence Jennings began working for the family in 1920, when young Alice was thirteen. Miss Jennings was hired primarily to care for Florence Ingersoll's daily needs, and to assist her with the many responsibilities and tasks involved in running the household – tasks that were becoming more and more overwhelming for Florence all the time. With Miss Jennings' help, things ran smoothly, even though the mistress of the house rarely left her bedroom.

Alice, an energetic and spirited teenager, resented Miss Jennings' presence in her home, however. She didn't like it when Miss Jennings told her to be quiet and not run in the house. She didn't like it when Miss Jennings told her not to go into her Mother's room, because her Mother was resting. She didn't like her. What right did Miss Jennings have to tell her what to do? She was not in charge of her. It may have been that Alice would not have liked any stranger who moved into their home. Florence Jennings was not a house guest. She was a permanent member of the household with her own room. She was a person who had in many ways become a part of the family. She had been hired to help her Mother, but Alice never felt that Florence Jennings had the right to boss her around. She felt that she should be free to see her mother whenever she wanted to. Sometimes she just needed to tell her Mother about something that had happened at school; sometimes she had a problem she wanted help solving; sometimes she just needed a hug.

Alice had always been very close to her father, but he worked long hours at the Company. Sometimes he even came home late for dinner. Her time with him was very limited, especially during the week. To make things worse, Alice's sister, Rachel, six years older, was now off at college and living in Boston. Young Alice did not even have the comfort of her older sister's presence to help ease the difficult adjustment. She needed her Mother.

Alice — Part 2

Sixteen-year-old Alice did, in time, accept Miss Jennings' presence. Alice learned to accept her presence because Alice was strong, because she was positive, and because she was a born survivor. She accepted, but she never really learned to truly care for or even to appreciate her mother's caregiver.

Florence Jennings had been living with the family for four years when the decision was made to remove Florence Ingersoll's spleen – a surgery that promised hope of ending her depression, and restoring the joy to her life. She was there when Robert returned from the hospital with the devastating news that his wife had had a post-operative hemorrhage and —had died. She was there when Alice burst into the house at 3:20 pm, anxious for news of her Mother. She was there when Alice in her grief locked herself into the front hall closet.

Now she would have to leave. She had lived with the Ingersoll family, and been Florence's companion for almost four years, but now her job was over. With Florence Ingersoll's death, there was nothing more that Miss Jennings could do to help the family.

Robert encouraged her to stay until after memorial service to help with all the funeral arrangements. After that her services were no longer needed. The day after the funeral, she cleaned out her room, packed up her belongings, and moved in with her sister. Her plan was to stay with her sister while she looked for a new position.

THE INGERSOLL HOUSE WAS NOW VERY, VERY QUIET. VERY quiet that is except for young Alice and the whirlwinds of activity that often accompanied her presence. Alice came home from school now with no one to greet her except the servants. There was no one with whom to share the adventures of her day. Robert was very sensitive to young Alice's grief, and made a special effort to be home in time for dinner every night, so he and his daughter could have that special time together each evening. He missed Miss Jennings, however, and her warm, friendly presence. The house felt very, very empty with both Florences gone.

"I'll just give her a call," he thought. "I'll ring her up and see how she is doing."

Ring her up he did, and also invited her to take a walk with him the following weekend. Florence Jennings and Robert Ingersoll began seeing each other almost every weekend to walk, to have dinner, or to see a show. In time, they realized that they had fallen in love. He asked her to marry him. She accepted, but they decided that it would be best to wait to get married until after Alice had graduated from high school.

Alice graduated from high school in June, 1926. Her father and Florence Jennings were married a few weeks later, and on July 15, Florence moved back into the Ingersoll home.

Mother never completely accepted her step-mother. Apparently, Florence cleaned out my mother's room after she went off to college. According to Mother, Florence got rid of all Mother's toys, including her dolls, without asking her first. It made her very sad. Mother never developed a meaningful relationship with her step-mother. I think as she matured, however, she learned to understand her father's caring for his second wife, and the comfort and happiness Florence Jennings brought to the father she loved so deeply.

1926

ALICE GRADUATED FROM CENTRAL HIGH SCHOOL IN Springfield in June, 1926. She had been accepted at a two-year finishing school in Boston, the Garland School of Homemaking, and was off to the big city. Her sister, Rachel, six years older, was already living and working in Boston. Having Rachel nearby certainly must have helped Alice with the transition.

After completing the two-year course of study at the Garland School of Homemaking, Alice worked for the next two years as a buyer for R.H. White's department store, a job she thoroughly enjoyed. Garland School then became accredited as a junior college. When that happened, Alice decided that this was her opportunity to get her degree. She was accepted at Boston University, and paid for room and board at the Garland School, which was within walking distance of BU.

Alice completed her Bachelor's degree in Education in two years, and then took another retail job, this time as a buyer at Filene's, where she was soon promoted to the training department. With the promotion came a little pink slip that said, "This is to notify you that your salary has been increased from $18.00 a week to $25.00 a week." She often wished that she had saved that little pink slip!

Garland Junior College no longer exists today. It was absorbed by Simmons College in 1976.

SEPTEMBER, 1934

IT WAS A WARM SATURDAY EVENING IN LATE SEPTEMBER of 1934. The maple trees along Commonwealth Avenue were just beginning to change color, and there a slight hint of fall was in the air.

Alice slipped into the yellow, flower print dress that she had bought on sale last week in Filenes' basement. She loved the stylish length and the soft flow of the skirt. The color, she knew, was a perfect accent to her attractive, brown eyes. Her date should be here any minute to pick her up. Just enough time for one last check to be sure her slip wasn't showing, and then she would be ready to go. Their plan was to go out for a bite to eat, and then see the new film at the Brattle Theater, "It Happened One Night" starring Clark Gable.

Ten minutes went by, then twenty minutes, and still no sign of her date. What could have happened? They had gone out several times before, and he had never before been late. Alice waited a little by longer, and then decided to drive over to the Harvard Law School dorm to see if she could find out what happened.

As she drove down Memorial Drive towards Harvard Square, her brain churned with possibilities. Was he sick? Had his car broken down? She pulled up in front of the dorm, parked the car, and then darted up the front steps to the dorm office. Picking up the phone, she dialed his room number. "Hello" said the familiar, male voice on the other end of the line.

"Hi", said Alice. "What happened? I waited for you for more than half an hour".

"Oh, was our date tonight? I thought we had plans to go out next weekend", he replied.

"Well, if we go now, we could still make it to the movie on time, and then we could get something to eat afterwards", said Alice.

"Er-rr, well, no. I can't do that." he said. " I have other plans tonight. I will call you next week."

Disappointed and angry, Alice lost her temper, and began to tell him in no uncertain terms how upset she felt. As far as she was concerned, he was standing her up. At this very moment, Jim, a lean, handsome law student was walking by at the top of the stairs above the office. He couldn't help but overhear everything that Alice said as she lost her temper, and bawled out her date.

"Who is this girl?" He thought to himself. "I like her spirit and her spunk."

Curious to see for himself, he went downstairs to the office to meet her. He liked what he saw. They chatted for a short while, and before Alice left, Jim had not only gotten her phone number, but had also asked her for a date for the following weekend.

James Hoffman and Alice Ingersoll met that September evening in the lobby of the Harvard Law School dorm. Six months later he asked her to marry him. She was 27 years old and he was 24. Since Alice's mother was dead, and her relationship with her step-mother was tenuous, at best, they decided that the wise thing to do would be to elope. In neighboring New Hampshire it was possible to get a marriage license after just a one week waiting period. They were married in Nashua, New Hampshire on March 1, 1935. Alice had just gotten a 39 percent pay increase at Filene's in March. Two months later, in June, Jim graduated from Harvard Law School and was hired by Sullivan and Cromwell, a prestigious law firm in New York. They were off to the big city!! Alice did not have long to enjoy her generous new pay check.

Who was Jim Hoffman? James was the second child and second son of Charles and Agnes Hoffman of Baltimore, Maryland. Dr. Charles Hoffman was a surgeon at Johns Hopkins Hospital in Baltimore, and Agnes was an attentive, if not possibly, an overly doting mother to James, his older brother Charles, Jr, and his younger sister Mary. The boys were both expected to do well in school, and to pursue careers in either medicine or law. Mary Edith, the daughter, and quite possibly the brightest and best student, was not encouraged to prepare for a profession or even to go to college. Women at that time were expected only to be homemakers. In her words, "Planning for a career would only result in taking jobs away from the men."

I have always had an extremely high regard for my "Aunt Mimi" in every way – intellectually, morally, and spiritually. Growing up as I did with the assumption that I would of course go to college, I often wondered whether or not she had any regrets or resentments about the opportunities that she had missed. One day I finally mustered up enough courage to broach the subject. It was hard for me, because I did not want to hurt her feelings or possibly risk her thinking that I was being judgmental in any way. To my surprise, and in some ways to my relief, she responded quite matter-of-factly that it would be wrong for a woman to take jobs away from men. The men needed the higher paying jobs in order to support their families. There was no indication that she felt any thing other than this was just the way things were. She thought this was right.

1936

ALICE AND JIM SET UP HOUSEKEEPING IN A SMALL, BUT charming walk-up apartment on Christopher Street in Greenwich Village. This historic area on the west side of Manhattan, commonly called The Village, consisted of narrow, curved streets lined by low to mid-rise brick apartments and 19th century row houses. It stood in sharp contrast to the high-rise landscape in most of the city. The young couple spent many lazy weekend afternoons exploring the local art galleries and the intriguing antique shops in their neighborhood.

These carefree early-married days were short-lived, however. Five months after they moved to New York City and nine months after they got married, Alice discovered that she was pregnant. Their apartment was too cramped for another person, even a very small person, and the neighborhood itself was not a welcoming place for young children. With a baby on the way, they decided to look for a modest house on Long Island. It would not be too far for Jim to commute and would provide a much better environment to raise a child.

They found a small house on a quiet street in Douglaston that was just perfect, and moved in the spring of 1936. Alice had time to paint the baby's room, put up curtains, find a crib, and generally make their home ready for the new arrival. Jim's sister, Mary Edith, was living in Baltimore, but she would come to Douglaston quite often on the train to visit for a week or two.

As Alice's due date drew closer, and then passed, her doctor expressed concerns. He feared that it could possibly be an unusually difficult labor and birth. When Alice told Jim that evening what the doctor had said, Jim immediately called his father, a gynecologist in Baltimore, for advice.

"What do you think, Dad?" asked Jim. "What should we do?"

"Have Alice come to Baltimore," said Dr. Hoffman. "I will deliver the baby myself. She can stay here with us until the baby comes. We have plenty of room, and Mother and I would love to have her. Mother also thinks it would be wise for Mary Edith to accompany her to Baltimore. See if she can take the time off from work." Three days later Alice and Mary Edith boarded the train to Baltimore – a three-hour trip.

The two young women arrived in Baltimore and quickly settled in on the second floor in the guest room in Mary Edith's girlhood home. As guests in a home with a live-in maid, as well as a laundress who came three days a week, there was very little for the two young women to do to help around the house. They spent long, leisurely afternoons visiting friends of Mary Edith's, and spending time with her dear mother. Five days later at 1:00 am, Alice's labor pains started. "Wake up," she whispered to Mary Edith, who was sleeping next to her in the same bed. "My contractions have started." Mary Edith jumped out of bed and went across the hall to wake up her father. Dr. Hoffman groggily rolled out of bed and ambled over to Alice's room. After giving her a quick look, he said, "It will be awhile yet. Let's wait until morning. You two try to get some sleep."

Did he really think that Alice would be able to go back to sleep? Granddaddy Hoffman may have delivered a lot of babies, but he obviously was unaware of what it was actually like for a woman in labor. Maybe Mother would have been able to doze off a bit from time to time, but actually sleep? I don't think so!!

Dr. Hoffman quickly fell back to sleep, but Alice and Mary Edith did not. They spent the rest of the night giggling, talking, and waiting for Alice's contractions – contractions that gradually became stronger and closer together. The next morning the whole family awoke at daybreak, dressed quickly, and headed for the hospital.

As feared, the delivery was long and difficult. At one point a young intern suggested crushing the baby's head to save the life of the mother. This was not an uncommon practice at the time. Dr. Hoffman said, "No." He felt confident that with a little more time and patience his first grandchild would be delivered safely. He was right. Mary Alice Hoffman was finally born in the early afternoon of October 23rd. The labor lasted more than 24 hours, and her head was noticeably misshapen from the forceps. Caesarian births were known at that time, but were still very rare.

Alice needed time to recuperate from the difficult birth. She spent the usual two weeks in the hospital, followed by three more weeks with her in-laws before she, baby Mary Alice, and Mary Edith boarded the train on November 30 to go back home to Douglaston.

During that time in Baltimore, Alice read Margaret Mitchell's novel, *Gone With the Wind*, which had been published earlier that year. Alice found the book so engrossing she could hardly put it down. Fortunately, she had a flashlight that she used to read under the covers after the lights had been turned off for the night at the hospital.

Perhaps Mother gained some comfort from the knowledge that her first childbirth experience had not been nearly as traumatic as Melanie Wilkes' had been, or perhaps she realized that she too had a sister-in-law just as loyal as Melanie. Perhaps it was both!

The fact that Jim did not go to Baltimore with Mother, but stayed at home, and continued to go to work, would not have been thought of as unusual. Husbands were not allowed in the delivery room in those days, and his presence would only have been seen as being in the way.

1937

Life with a new baby was an adjustment for Alice, as it is for all new mothers. Her doctor encouraged her to get little Mary Alice on a schedule as soon as possible, but a feeding schedule was not a part of Mary Alice's agenda. She was an alert, active baby and found being awake much more interesting than sleeping. When she was awake, crying was one of her favorite activities. Any free moments that were not devoted to Mary Alice's needs, were spent addressing the constant collection of baby bottles to be washed and sterilized. The bottles were boiled on the kitchen stove in a large pot of water with a wire rack inside designed to keep them safely upright. There was also the never-ending pile of dirty diapers to be washed in the wonderful, new Bendix washing machine and then hung outside on the clothes line to dry. The diapers also needed to be boiled on the stove from time to time to help prevent the ever-present threat of diaper rash.

Eventually Alice's days began to take on some

small semblance of a routine, but she did not have anywhere near as much time or energy to entertain or plan the social events that Jim so enjoyed, and had come to expect. Alice loved to cook, and she also loved to entertain, so the demands of her expected social role in supporting Jim's career were not in themselves a huge burden. But, now with a new baby to care for, an especially active one as well, Alice found planning and putting on dinner parties much more challenging. Jim was proud of his new daughter, however. She looked like the Hoffman side of the family, and had his green eyes, blond hair, and fair coloring. A baby boy would have been his first choice, but he drew comfort in knowing that in time they would certainly have another child.

That time was to come sooner than either of them expected. When Mary Alice was just seven months old, and life had finally begun to assume some kind of predictable rhythm, Alice discovered that she was pregnant again. Her first reaction when she heard the news was to burst out in tears. How could she even think about another baby? She wasn't ready physically, she wasn't ready emotionally. The thought of another child was completely overwhelming. Moreover the thought of the possibility of facing another difficult birth was almost more that she could bear.

"I just don't know how I can do it," Alice said. "I can't go through another pregnancy again so soon. How will I ever be able to take care of two babies at the same time?"

"Well, it looks as if we do not have any choice," replied Jim. "We will just have to do the best we can. It won't be a problem financially, as you know, for I just got another generous raise last month. We will have to look for a bigger house, however. This cute little bungalow will be much too small."

A few months later, Alice, Jim and Mary Alice moved from Douglaston to a larger house, not more than three miles away, in Great Neck. The town of Great Neck was located on the north shore of Long Island on a peninsula, the first of many, that juts out into Long Island Sound. Jim could still easily commute on the train to the law firm in Manhattan. Alice bought a second crib and used any spare moments she had to get the new house ready for their expanding family. Jim pitched in to help with the endless projects on the weekends. Fortunately, Mary Alice would still stay in a playpen, but those days were numbered.

As her due date drew closer, Alice became concerned about how she would get to the hospital when the time came. The closest maternity hospital, the Woman's Hospital, was in upper Manhattan near the northwest corner of Central Park. It could take at best more than an hour to get there, depending on the traffic, and there was never any way to know whether or not Jim would even be home to drive her.

"Come stay with me," suggested her good friend, Edmay Seiter, who still lived in an apartment in Manhattan. "We don't have an extra bedroom, but you are more than welcome to sleep in the living room on the couch. John and I would love to have you. It would be fun."

Alice and Jim decided this would be a wise decision and jumped at the generous offer. Now all they would have to do is talk to the babysitter to find out if she could come a little earlier. Their favorite sitter had already promised to stay with Mary Alice during the day while Alice was in the hospital. Arrangements were soon made. Alice packed her suitcase, gave little Mary Alice a big hug good-bye, and headed into the city.

She felt a tremendous sense of relief knowing that the hospital was close by, and she would be able to get there quickly when her time came. It was hard for Alice to be away from her family, but it would be just a short while. The time was not short. Alice slept on her friend's living room couch for two full weeks before her contractions finally started! The wait was long, but fortunately the delivery was very quick. All her unspoken fears of another difficult delivery were unfounded. Sara was born on February 18, 1938 – a cold, sunny day in Manhattan – a healthy baby girl. Again Jim did not get his hoped-for boy.

Alice spent the customary two weeks in the hospital before finally going home to Great Neck. She had not seen sixteen-month-old, little Mary Alice for four weeks!

1938-1939

Iт was a clear, sunny day in early March, 1938, when Alice, with baby Sara in her arms, left Women's Hospital in New York City. Jim had taken the day off to drive his wife and brand new daughter home to Great Neck. As their car turned into the driveway, they saw little Mary Alice peering expectantly out the living room window.

"Mommy, Mommy," she called excitedly as her parents came into the house.

Alice passed the infant to Jim, and kneeled down to give Mary Alice a big hug. Her busy little toddler looked so much older and more grown up than she had been the day Alice said good-bye to her nearly a month ago. There would be no way to recapture the time she had missed, but it would not take Alice very long to discover all the new things that Mary Alice had learned during the time they were apart – new words, new motor skills, new tricks. She still had a bottle and she still wore diapers, but Mary Alice was a big, big girl compared to the toddler she had left behind four weeks before, and certainly huge compared to baby Sara.

To Alice's great surprise and delight Sara was an unusually easy baby. She slept well between feedings, and was content and happy during her wakeful times. Life with both a newborn and a toddler was certainly challenging, but not as over-whelming as Alice had feared.

She may not have been a planned baby, or better yet, the hoped for boy, but she won them over by learning very early how to get her needs met with-out unnecessarily ruffling too many feathers.

This expanding household was soon to wel-come yet another family member. Jim's younger sister, Mary Edith, who was still living at home with her parents in Baltimore, had recently broken her engagement. She felt a need for the first time to leave her childhood home – a need for a change of scene, and an opportunity for new experiences.

"Mimi, we have this great big house with extra bedrooms. Why don't you come live with us?" Jim suggested. "I don't think you would have any trouble finding a job in New York City. There are job openings listed in the paper every day. You could drive to the train station with me in the morn-ing," said Jim, "and I would certainly enjoy having company on my daily commute." Mary Edith had always felt close to her brother, and she and Alice had become good friends. She agreed to come and stay with them. Jim was right. Mary Edith found a job at the New York Stock Exchange two weeks after she arrived. Alice was thrilled having her sister-in-law and dear friend living with them.

Mary Edith soon found that she loved living in Great Neck, but the commute to the city was tiring and unpleasant. She decided to give up the daily commute to New York City, and look for a job in Great Neck. She answered an ad for a sales-clerk position at the local music shop, and was hired on the spot. Being both a quick learner and unusually personable, it was not long before the music shop owner noticed that his business had increased considerably. One of the frequent customers was an attractive young bachelor who started finding more and more excuses to stop by the shop. Fred Pearce finally found the courage to ask Mary Edith for a date.

Three months later on September 9, 1939, they were married. The wedding was in Great Neck at St. Paul's Episcopal Church located directly across the street from the house where Fred had grown up, and where his parents still lived. The church was filled!! Mary Edith wore a tailored street length aqua dress, and a fashionable, large brimmed fabric hat to match. Alice was not only the maid of honor, but the reception was at Alice and Jim's house. Alice was the hostess for this special family event as well. Fortunately, the weather cooperated. It was a glorious day, allowing the 100 wedding guests to enjoy food and drink not only inside the house, but outside in the garden as well.

Children were not invited to the wedding, but an exception was made for almost three year-old Mary Alice, and nineteen months-old Sara. The party was at their house, and some might say they stole the show.

Old Court House Road – 1940

ONE SUNDAY WHILE PERUSING THE PAPER, JIM'S EYE was caught by an advertisement in the real estate section. "For Rent – one half of old Long Island farmhouse on three acres. Included are four bedrooms, living room, dining room, kitchen and bath." Jim was intrigued by the ad, was curious as it was certainly not the kind of ad that one came across every day.

"Let's drive over there and take a look at it," Jim suggested.

"Why not?" replied Alice. "Give me a minute to get the girls ready."

Less than a half hour later, Alice and Jim turned into a long driveway that led up a gentle slope to a circular drive near the house. They soon noticed that, in addition to the house itself, there was also a hay barn, a three car garage, a chicken house, and a pond on this unpretentious property. The property was situated, however, between two very large homes that were not only very pretentious, they were gated. Fortunately, the large gated homes were not even visible from the road.

Alice and Jim quickly introduced themselves to the owners and were given a tour of the part of the house that was for rent. They liked what they saw. They liked the owners, they liked the house, and they fell in love with all the open space surrounding it.

It was with mixed emotions, however, that Alice moved from the lovely home that she and Jim owned in Great Neck to this historic farmhouse on Old Court House Road in New Hyde Park. Jim felt strongly that in spite of the longer commute into the city each day, the opportunity to have a vegetable garden, and the huge, outdoor space for the children to play, far outweighed any disadvantages.

Alice was soon won over as well. Instead of being on a street lined with houses, the girls had trees to climb, grassy slopes to roll down, a pond for stone skipping, a hay barn to explore, and chickens to feed.

As soon as the family was settled, Jim set to work on weekends, with spade and hoe, preparing the soil for his vegetable garden (which a year later was to become a victory garden). Any rocks were removed and the earth was raked smooth. Rows were planted with lettuce, carrots, and peas, and a section set aside for pole beans and tomatoes. Mary Alice and Sara, aged four and three, were not considered old enough to help with the planting, but old enough to help with the weeding. Jim taught them how to thin the carrots, identify weeds, and how to work without stepping on the precious plants. He was somewhat of a task master.

The vegetable garden thrived and produced a bountiful harvest. Even after sharing with friends and neighbors, it was more than they could eat. Alice had never done any canning before. She had never needed to. She needed to now.

The owner, who lived in the other half of the house, had been canning for many years, and was more than happy to teach Alice. Aunt Florence, as she was affectionately called, showed her the canning jars to buy. She explained the kind of stainless steel canning pot she would need, complete with a wire rack to keep each jar upright in the pot.

And can Alice did! She canned tomatoes, she canned green beans, and she canned carrots. At the end of a busy canning day, a field of sanitized jars with sealed lids lined the kitchen counter.

Barbara was born on April 4th, 1941. Mary Alice remembers Barbara as a child better than I do. Her first memory is of placing the still-crawling Barbara as a toddler in a wagon and rolling her down a small hill. Because we elder daughters were so close in age Barbara seemed much younger. We had little to do with her, as she was the baby.

Aunt Florence

THE OWNERS OF THIS FARMHOUSE ON Old Court House Road were Florence and Bill Trites. The house and the three acres of land had been in Florence's family since the early 1820s. It had been built by her great-grandfather, Richard Williams, a descendent of one of the original settlers of Hempstead, Long Island. She herself was born in the house, and had lived there all her life. Florence Williams Trites willed the house in her estate to New York State. The house is now part of the Old Bethpage Village Restoration in central Long Island.

"Please call us Aunt Florence and Uncle Bill," said Florence shortly after we moved in, and we did. They always seemed like family. In fact, they were like grandparents to us. Later I was to learn that everyone in the community called her Aunt Florence.

Aunt Florence was fifty years old when she and Uncle Bill married, so she never had any children of her own. She loved children, however, and we three little girls always felt welcome on their side of the house. In fact we roamed back and forth between the two houses as we pleased. The connecting doors were never locked.

I loved to go to Aunt Florence's house on the day she did her laundry. There was a modern Bendix washing machine in our kitchen, but Aunt Florence still did her weekly laundry in her out-kitchen or shed, just as she had all her life. First she made a wood fire in the big beehive oven to heat the water in a caldron suspended over the flames. The hot water was then carefully scooped and poured into her new electric washing tub that gyrated back and forth when turned on. She carefully sorted her cloths into whites and coloreds. If any stains needed special attention, she scrubbed them on a washboard before placing them in the machine. While the machine jostled the clothes, Aunt Florence ladled water into two wooden rinse tubs – one with bluing. These rinse tubs were at waist height, either on a bench or with wooden legs.

After washing the clothes, Aunt Florence put them though a wringer. The wringer had wooden rollers and a hand crank to turn it. Next the clean clothes were placed into the rinse tubs. Whites went into the tub with bluing. After being thoroughly rinsed, she put the clothes through the hand wringer one more time before pinning them with wooden clothes pins to a rope clothes line in the back yard. Hopefully the sun and wind would dry the clothes enough to be brought in before dark. In the winter it was not uncommon for the clothes to freeze before they were completely dry.

Even though my mother had a new washing machine, which both washed and rinsed the clothes, we too had a clothesline to hang them out to dry. No one had a clothes dryer at that time.

I liked to keep Aunt Florence company on wash day, but I didn't like to be nearby when she killed a chicken. There was a chicken house near the edge of the property with enough chickens to provide eggs for Aunt Florence and Uncle Bill, and for our family as well. Mary Alice and I were considered old enough not only to collect eggs from the nests, but also old enough to clean out the chicken house every few weeks. Removing dirty chicken-pooped straw, and replacing it with fresh, clean straw was never my favorite job, but, as I recall, we didn't complain.

From time to time, Aunt Florence took an unsuspecting chicken to the chopping block. I didn't like to watch the beheading, but once in awhile I'd be outside playing at the time and could not avoid the scene. She grabbed the poor chicken by its legs, and lifted it upside down. While still holding its legs tightly in her left hand, Aunt Florence would deftly lay the chicken's head on the chopping block – an old tree stump in the side yard. In her right hand was an axe. With one quick stroke of the axe, the head was cut off. Blood sprayed everywhere as Aunt Florence dropped the chicken to the ground. The beheaded bird then jumped up onto its feet and started running around in circles. After several minutes, it finally it fell to the ground dead. The next chore for Aunt Florence was the time consuming process of plucking the chicken. Each feather had to be pulled out one by one before the chicken could then be cleaned, dressed and ready to cook.

I can still picture those startled, beheaded chickens running aimlessly around in circles. It was hard for me to accept that my loving, nurturing Aunt Florence was the source of their final fate. I never had the good fortune to know my maternal grandmother, Florence Ingersoll, since she died when my mother was just seventeen years old. Another Florence came along, however, and took her place in my heart.

ALICE AND JIM HAD MOVED NOT MORE THAN A FEW MILES from their old neighborhood, so friends could easily come for parties and gatherings on the weekends – and entertain they did. Jim liked to be the center of attention, and as party host he was in his element. One of his favorite antics was to step up on a chair holding a glass of water and a broom. Placing the glass of water up against the ceiling, he would then position the end of the broom handle up against the bottom of the glass. After he had stepped down and the chair was removed, he would ask an unsuspecting guest to please hold the broom handle for him. Once he had a taker, he walked away!

I especially remember one outdoor summer party. I must have been five or six years old. I was having fun riding my tricycle around the large, circular driveway, and watching the people. Daddy called me to come in and get ready for bed. "Why should I go in?" I thought. "The sun is still shining, the people are still here, and I am having fun. "No," I said to myself, "I won't go in." Little by little, as the sun slowly sank in the west, the guests began to leave. Feeling ready for bed, I cheerfully headed toward the front door. Daddy was standing in the doorway. He would not let me in. "No problem," I thought, "I'll go in the side door." When I arrived at the side door, there Daddy stood. He would not let me in. Undeterred, I hurried to the back door. There he was again. I then scurried to Aunt Florence's back door, her side door, *and her front door,* only to be faced each time by Daddy yet again, unwilling to let me in. I had been all the way around the house, and back again to our front door. Daddy finally let me in, but not without a swift spank on the rear end.

Daddy was also very strict about bedtime. Once you were in bed, had said your prayers, and the lights were out, there was no getting up for any reason. We also knew that he could easily hear us, if we did get up. The house was old, and the wide floor boards creaked when you stepped on them. I soon discovered, however, that in the hallway between my bedroom and the bathroom, there was one board that did not creak. It was the board right next to the wall. I learned that if I walked foot over foot on just that board, I could get safely to the bathroom and back without being discovered. It was the perfect plan. If I got caught, I knew I would be spanked, but I also knew I would be spanked if I wet the bed.

Our house had only one bathroom, which was not uncommon at that time. Everyone shared. We also shared Daddy's comb, which he kept in the medicine cabinet. He didn't mind sharing, but would get very angry if we would take his comb and not return it. This happened frequently, and usually resulted in a spanking. Why we didn't have more than one comb is a mystery.

But Daddy could also be playful and fun, in addition to being strict and demanding. He told us that we never had to worry about his having a flat tire. There were elves riding on his front bumper always looking for any nails or tacks on the road. The elves would pick up any they saw, and keep him safe. At Christmas time, in addition to the usual cookies and milk for Santa, he would go outside and ring sleigh bells. In the morning he would ask us if we had heard Santa's bells during the night. We always answered, "Yes."

He was a meticulous dresser, and laid out his clothes for work the next day on the chaise lounge in their bedroom—his suit, tie, shirt, belt, socks, and on the floor, his shoes. He wanted to make sure they all went together. On fall mornings he would come out the door on his way to work, and pick a fringed gentian from a bed of flowers in front of the house. It was soon stuck in his suit lapel button hole. I can still picture him doing this. It must have lifted his spirits, as often he would whistle as he did it.

Exploring

"GIRLS, GO OUTSIDE AND PLAY," SAID ALICE. "I'LL call you when it is time for lunch. Daddy is out doing some errands, but he should be home soon."

"Let's play the toll road game," said five-year-old Mary Alice. "Yes, let's," said four-year-old Sara. "I'll get the rope from the closet." She grabbed the rope, and the two girls quickly ran out the front door and down the grassy front lawn to the street.

Old Court House Road was a country road with very little traffic. The only cars belonged to the few neighbors who lived a quarter of a mile away, or to the occasional visitors or service people. A shallow, bubbling brook ran parallel to Old Court House Road on the other side of the street. Between the road and the brook was a split rail fence with a wide, flat board along the top. One of the girls' favorite past times was to gingerly walk, foot over foot, along the top of the split rail fence–balancing very carefully and trying not to fall. Fall they would from time to time. It was inevitable, but that was part of the adventure, if not part of the fun. Today they were not going to walk along the top of the split rail fence. They were going to play "toll road".

As soon as they got to the street at the bottom of the hill, Mary Alice crossed to the other side of the road holding one end of the rope. Sara stayed on the grass holding the other end. They pulled the rope tight. Their toll station was in place, and now they just had to wait for a car.

Soon a car approached. When the driver saw the children, he slowed, and when he saw the rope stretched across the street, he came to a full stop.

"Five cents toll, five cents toll," Mary Alice and Sara called out in unison. The driver smiled, reached into his pocket and pulled out a shiny new nickel. The rope was lowered, and the car continued on its way. During the next half hour three or four more cars approached, stopped, and then willing paid the five cents toll.

"Here comes another car," cried Mary Alice. "Pull the rope tight." The car came to a stop, and who should the driver be but Jim. "Daddy," said Mary Alice, "Where did you get this car? It is beautiful! Whose is it?"

"It's ours now," said Jim. "I bought it this morning. We needed another car, so your mother wouldn't have to drive me to the train station every day. I hope she won't be mad. I think you two better stop playing in the road. It is not a good idea. Hop in, and you can ride up to the house with me in our new car."

When Alice heard a car coming up the driveway, she looked out the window, and saw Jim and the girls in the shiny new pale green Lincoln Zephyr. She knew Jim had always dreamed of owning a convertible, but buying a brand new car – a Lincoln, no less, seemed way out of line. What could he have been thinking? Alice was not pleased with his expensive decision, but the Lincoln Zephyr was here to stay.

A month later Grandma Hoffman arrived from Baltimore for a two-week visit. Jim adored his mother, and was excited as he drove to the train station in his new car to meet her. It was a warm, sunny day, so he was able to have the top down as he showed off his pride and joy.

The next morning Mary Alice and Sara stayed inside for awhile to spend time with Grandma, but soon got restless, and went out to play. They swung on the swing, rode their bikes around the driveway, and then decided to explore. Exploring was one of their favorite things to do.

"Let's explore the garage," said Sara. We've never looked at all the things in there."

"Look at all the cans of paint," said Mary Alice as they walked into the garage. There was a whole wall of shelves stacked high with partly used cans. "I wonder what we could paint," she thought. "Daddy's new car is not a very pretty color. That grey green is boring. Red is my favorite color. I think he would like it much better if his car were red. Look, I see some red paint up on the top shelf. I think I can get it."

Sara watched as Mary Alice climbed onto the workbench, and then reached up to the top shelf for the can of red paint. Soon they found some brushes, opened the paint can with a screwdriver, and started to paint. They were excited. Daddy would be so pleased.

"I haven't heard the girls for awhile," Grandma said to Alice. "Do you think they are all right?"

"Oh, I am sure they are just fine," answered Alice. "Don't worry."

"Well, let me just take a look," replied Grandma. "I'll find out what they are doing."

"Mary Alice, Sara, where are you?" called Grandma as she passed the garage and headed toward the barn.

Hearing her call, the girls dropped their paint-brushes and ran out of the garage.

"Oh, merciful heavens," exclaimed Grandma when she saw them. "You're bleeding! You're bleeding! Whatever happened?"

Hearing Grandma Hoffman's anxious cries,

Aunt Florence came running out of her house to see what the matter was. It soon became clear that what Grandma feared to be blood was not blood at all. It was only red paint—the girls were covered with bright red paint! Feeling relieved, Grandma and Aunt Florence headed back to the house with the two girls in tow. Aunt Florence grabbed a big can of turpentine from the garage on the way. The girls were stripped. One went into Aunt Florence's tub. One went into their own tub. Their clothes were soaked in turpentine, their hair was washed with turpentine, and all signs of red paint were finally removed from their hands, arms, and faces. Spanking was the usual result of any infraction, but in this case the sense of relief that the little girls were not bleeding was so great that initially no one even thought about a punishment. But there was more to come. Jim had not yet seen the car.

When Jim came in from working in his Victory garden and discovered what had happened, he was livid. He was so angry that he turned white, and blue veins stuck out on the side of his face. He gave the girls the dickens, but with his mother visiting, this time the girls were spared the spanking they were due.

1945

To the casual observer Alice and Jim had an ideal marriage. He was doing unusually well professionally; they had three healthy children, many good friends, and had been minimally affected by the economic depression and the war. Jim was proud of his family, but often had difficulty interacting with more than one child at a time.

He loved to bike, and often would go for short bike rides on the weekends. At Mother's encouragement, he would take one of us with him, and we would sit in front of him on the bar of the bike- no helmet, of course. Since there was only room for one child, Mary Alice was usually the one who got to go – probably because she was the oldest. I have very few memories of doing anything with Daddy one on one.

When they only had one car, Alice would drive Jim to the train station two days a week, so that she could have the car to shop and do errands. After she had fed the girls in the early evening, Alice would pick Jim up at the train station. The transition from work to family life was usually softened by stopping on the way home at his favorite cocktail lounge in Lake Success. He and Alice would have a cocktail, and the girls were treated to a delicious scoop of vanilla bean ice cream in a shiny silver dish. This was would be their family time. By the time they finally arrived home it would be time for the little girls to go to bed.

I always liked the scoop of vanilla bean ice cream – that was the best part– but I never enjoyed the hour or more that my parents spent having a cocktail at this dimly lit bar filled with grown-ups and strangers. I just wanted to go home. They always talked about things that I did not understand, and I don't ever remember being included in the conversation.

OVER TIME JIM BECAME MORE AND MORE SWEPT UP WITH the glamour and excitement of his work. Success had come easily, but in spite of doing well, he was constantly reaching to do even more. He was unusually driven to prove himself to be better than anyone else, and to move up in the firm. Work took over. More and more frequently there would be late afternoon calls home to say that he still had more work to do, and would not be home for dinner. The workload was always his excuse.

There were legal secretaries at Jim's office, as there are at any law firm. One particular young woman began to work late on many of the same evenings that Jim was putting in extra hours at the office. She was young, she was sexy, and Jim was not oblivious to her charms. He began to feel young and carefree again when he was with Joan on these evenings at the office, and soon wanted to spend more and more time with her. It was not long before he realized that he was falling in love. He wanted to marry Joan. He wanted a divorce.

Neither my sister Mary Alice nor I have any memories of our parents arguing, of our mother crying, or of anything else that would indicate unusual conflict between our parents. They both clearly must have made a concerted effort to protect all three of us from the stress and conflict that existed between them.

THIS WAS IN THE MID 1940S. MARRIAGE WAS VIEWED AS the normal condition of the American adult. The women's magazines at that time offered abundant evidence that marriage was a problem for women to solve. It was a relationship fraught with difficulties that were primarily the task of the woman to negotiate and overcome. It was a rare issue of a woman's magazine that did not offer ways to rejuvenate or patch up a marriage. The popular column "Can This Marriage Be Saved" began in the *Ladies Home Journal* in the early 1940's. It was the majority view at that time that if a marriage failed, it was the woman's fault. Articles encouraged women to be realistic about marriage and work on their relationships. Alice certainly tried hard to follow the rules and suggestions, but the cards were stacked against her.

Since Jim was a lawyer, he was well aware of all the legal hurdles and options. Divorce was fault-based in the 1940's, so to avoid being ruled the one at fault and to have to pay alimony, Jim's first plan was to try to prove that Alice was an unfit mother. Any mother who could not adequately care for her children because of alcohol or drug addiction, mental illness, sexual abuse, neglect or abandonment was considered an unfit mother. This was certainly a desperate attempt on his part, and was completely unrealistic. In no way was Alice an unfit mother. After that failed attempt, the only possible legal route was to get a divorce. Alice would have to be convinced to divorce him based on adultery.

"If you will not divorce me," said Jim, "I will make your life miserable forever."

"What choice do I have," Alice thought sadly to herself. A divorce was not what she ever wanted, but living in a one-sided marriage would be even worse.

Mother must have told Daddy that since he was the one that wanted the divorce, he would have to be the one to tell the girls. I have a very vivid memory of Daddy and I sitting at the kitchen table, and his telling me that he would not be living with us anymore. He explained that he and Mother no longer wanted to be married. He would be moving out of the house, but he would come visit us frequently. I was stunned, and do not remember saying much of anything in reply. Mary Alice was certainly told as well, but she has no memory of it. Was she in denial?

THE ONLY ACCEPTED GROUNDS FOR DIVORCE AT THE TIME were cruelty, desertion or adultery. Alice would have to sue Jim for divorce based on adultery. In New York State, where they lived, the wait time to get a divorce was twelve months, but there were other states where the wait time was much shorter. In fact, in Nevada, it was only six weeks.

"I don't want to wait for twelve months," said Jim, "not when you can get a divorce now in Nevada in just six weeks. I think you should go to Nevada and establish residency, so we get this over with as quickly and easily as possible."

Arrangements were soon made for Alice to take the train to Las Vegas, Nevada. She would stay with a woman who rented rooms in her home to people needing a place to live while they were waiting to become Nevada residents. Once you were a resident, you could get a divorce with no further wait. The amount of time required to establish residency in Nevada was originally six months, but was changed to only six weeks in 1931. Six weeks was certainly a short wait time for getting a divorce, but it was still a long time for Alice to be away from her children and her home – not to speak of the train trip, which must have added another week and a half. She boarded the train in early April, 1946, and the divorce decree was signed and filed in the eighth judicial district court of the state of Nevada on May 21, 1946.

Mother had never lived anywhere other than the northeastern part of the United States. It is hard to imagine what it must have been like for her leave her family, board a train all alone, and travel 2,500 miles away to live for six weeks with strangers in a totally unfamiliar environment. Two postcards that she sent to Mary Alice from Las Vegas provide a small window into her reaction to her new world. The first, dated April 24, 1946 said, "This is where I went to lunch last Thursday. It's a pretty ride through the desert. Everything is desert. It will be funny to be back home where there are tall green trees." The second, dated May 4, 1946, said, "This is one of the nice hotels in Las Vegas. Went here later in the evening last Saturday. It is fun to see all the people out having fun."

These two little post cards sent to my sister were clearly written by an open, positive spirit. Mother may have been down, but even in her darkest hour, she was not out. She often said, however, that if it hadn't been for us three girls, she did not know how she would have kept going.

1946

As Alice was struggling with the thoughts of traveling to Las Vegas to establish residency, and worrying about who would take care of her little girls while she was away, a most miraculous solution emerged! Mary Edith and Fred, her sister-in-law and brother-in-law, received a notice from their landlord. The owners needed the house. Mary Edith, Jim's sister, and Fred, her husband, would have to move out and find another place to live.

"Why don't you, Fred, and the children come live with me at the farm house," suggested Alice. "Since Fred has to travel so much for his work, you would not be all alone with your children when he is away, and I would love to have all of you with me."

"Yes, said Mary Edith, "and I could help you by taking care of the little girls while you are in Las Vegas. Also, by sharing the rent with you at the farm house, Fred and I might be able to save enough money for a down payment on a house of our own."

"It would make me feel so much less anxious," said Alice, "to know that you would be with the girls while I am away, Mary Edith. I know you love them almost as much as I do."

It was decided. Mary Edith, Fred and their two young children, Mimi and Ricky, ages 5 and 2, moved in with Alice and the girls at the farmhouse on Old Court House Road in New Hyde Park. The house comfortably housed them all. Jim had since moved out and was now living in an apartment in New York City with Joan, his secretary. He and Joan would marry as soon as Alice returned from Las Vegas and Jim and Alice's divorce was final.

While Alice was in Las Vegas, Mary Edith had five young children to care for all by herself – a nine-year-old, an eight-year old, two five-year olds, and a two-year-old. The older two girls were in school all day. The younger ones at home had not only cousins to play with, but also an enormous amount of outdoor space to explore.

Jim came out to visit Mary Edith and the children a couple of times during the two months that Alice was in Las Vegas. He brought Joan with him, and made sure that he came at a time when Fred was traveling for his work, so he would not be home. Fred would have had very little tolerance for Jim coming to visit the girls and bringing Joan with him.

Alice and Mary Edith had decided that it would be a wise idea to hire an ironing lady to come once a week to help keep up with the never ending cotton shirts, blouses, pants and dresses that had to be washed and pressed. Perma-press fabrics were not yet invented, or perhaps even dreamed of at that time. Mrs. Casmus started coming every Wednesday morning and soon became a special favorite with all the children. Every week without fail she brought a candy treat, usually Chuckles, Lifesavers or Necco Wafers, for the children.

WE LIKED THE CHUCKLES ESPECIALLY, WHICH WERE SIMILAR *to gum drops only larger, and we loved the word Chuckles. It always made us laugh.*

TWO MONTHS LATER WHEN ALICE RETURNED FROM LAS Vegas, her dear sister-in-law was there to greet her at the train station. Alice was not returning to the loneliness of a life by herself with her girls, but to an expanded household with other adults and other children. How very blessed she was.

THE UNEXPECTED GIFT

O N DECEMBER 27, 1946, WITH THEIR HEADS FILLED
with happy memories of Santa, Aunt Rachel,
Uncle Albert, cousins, and presents, Alice's three
little girls clambered into the car for the trip home.
They were reluctant to say good-bye, for it had
been a wonderful visit, and they did not know
when they would visit their mother's relatives
again. Donna, the black English setter, was already
happily perched in the back seat ready to go. "Me
first," shouted Mary Alice, as she hopped into the
front seat. Sara and Barbara, the two youngest, slid
in the back with the dog.

It had been the first Christmas since Alice's
unwanted divorce was final – the first Christmas
with only four stockings to hang at the chimney
instead of five. She had gratefully accepted her
sister Rachel's invitation to drive up to Massachusetts that year, and spend this especially painful
Christmas with her and her family.

The suitcases were loaded in the trunk, and
the newly unwrapped packages were nestled here

and there. Three brand new Radio Flyer sleds were securely tied onto the top of the car. After many "good-byes," Alice backed out of her sister's driveway and headed south. It was a crisp, cold day, but the traffic was light. With luck getting through the Bronx and across the Throgs Neck Bridge before the late afternoon traffic, the trip back home to Long Island wouldn't take more than three hours. The girls entertained themselves happily. A switch, as always, was hanging over the visor to handle any spats, if they should arise. As the car approached Bridgeport, there were radio reports of a storm headed up the coast toward New York City and western Long Island. This was a bit unsettling, but Alice felt that they should make it home safely before any snowfall.

Not long after, light flakes began to fall, and gradually became denser. By the time they reached the Bronx, the snow was falling so heavily that it was difficult to see more than a few feet ahead. Traffic moved slower and slower, and the sky gradually got darker and darker. Alice was concerned, and decided to find a place to stop. She pulled off the road at the first opportunity, and fortunately found an empty parking place in the snow-blanketed city. She parked in front of a pharmacy, and went inside to inquire about any possible places in the neighborhood to spend the night. While explaining her plight to the pharmacist, a nearby customer overheard their conversation.

"You can come and stay with me," the man said, "I live just upstairs". When she asked him his name, he answered, "Just call me Joe." Alice felt uncomfortable, so to reassure her, Joe said that he would go upstairs and get his wife. He came back in a few minutes with his wife, Mary, a small woman with kind eyes, who enthusiastically repeated the invitation.

Reassured, and with no other options, Alice, the three girls, and the dog trudged up the steep stairwell to Joe and Mary's apartment above the drug store. Meanwhile, Joe got the sleds off the roof of the car. Someone would undoubtedly lift them during the night if left behind.

Upstairs, they entered a small, but immaculate apartment. It was sparsely furnished, and in the corner of the living room stood a spindly Christmas tree with a meager assortment of gifts beneath it. Two shy but excited young children welcomed the visitors. "Are they going to stay with us?" the children asked. "Yes," their mother answered. Joe went to a neighbor to borrow a roll away bed. Two chairs were pushed together to make a bed for Barbara, the youngest. Mary Alice slept on the sofa, and Sara curled up in a sleeping bag on the floor. Everyone was safe and warm.

The next morning dawned bright and clear… the roads were plowed, and traffic through the city was moving again. Mary made a delicious breakfast of oatmeal, toast, and hot cocoa. The car was soon packed, Alice said good-bye and they headed for Long Island. They reached home in less than thirty minutes. They were stranded in the storm only twenty miles from home.

That night in the dark, after the children were asleep, Alice thought of Christmas at her sister's house – of the many new toys and gifts the children had received, and of the delicious dinner they had all enjoyed. Now she had met a family who have very few material possessions, but who opened their home and their hearts to her, a stranger, when she needed it the most. She was alone now. She was alone with three children to raise herself, but she would never be truly alone. She had her sister, she had her father, and she lived in a world with people like Joe and Mary, who knew the true meaning of Christmas.

1947

"QUIET DOWN! KEEP YOUR HANDS OFF EACH OTHER! If I have to speak to you one more time, I will stop the car and make you get out. You can walk home! Is that clear?"

Later Alice was sorry later that she had spoken so sharply to the girls. She knew that it was mostly her own stress that had caused her to lose her temper. She was finding it hard being a single parent. It was hard to have no one to help share the day-to-day responsibilities of caring for three active young children.

"I need to find a fun project to put my mind on," she thought. "I am enjoying the work as company sales representative that I am doing for the Milton Bradley Company, but I need a project that I can do at home—something I can do with my hands. A sewing project is what I need. I think I'll go to the fabric store tomorrow while the children are in school and look at the new pattern books."

The next morning she went down to the village shopping center as soon as the children had left for school, and the shops were open, to look at patterns. The new spring catalogues were in. It wasn't long before her eye fell on just the thing—a little girl's coat. Sara needed a new spring coat for Easter. This one would be perfect. She bought the pattern, and then started looking at fabrics. That was the part she really enjoyed. She soon found a light-weight wool in a subtle beige plaid. She bought the yardage needed, plus lining fabric, thread, and buttons.

After she got home, energized and excited, Alice laid out the fabric and carefully pinned the pattern pieces in place on the straight of the weave. She had everything pinned and ready to cut out before the girls arrived home from school. The next day she skillfully cut out each pattern piece with her newly sharpened pinking shears. The hardest part was done. Now the fun would begin. The fabric pieces were pinned, and then basted together. Sara had to stand very still while Alice had her try on each section before the final machine stitching.

"Don't wiggle! Stand up straight," said Alice. "Good!"

Now it was time to set up the sewing machine. Alice took her sewing table out of the closet, unfolded the legs, and placed the table in the corner of the dining room. The Singer Featherweight sewing machine dropped easily into the hole cut out for it in the table. Soon the machine was plugged in and ready to whir.

Alice deftly guided each seam through the sewing machine needle, keeping the stitch line straight and true. Each seam was then pressed open. Lastly the adjoining pattern pieces were stitched together. Sara's new Easter coat emerged little by little right before her delighted eyes.

It was a wonderful coat! The fabric was soft, it fit her perfectly, and best of all her mother had made it for her.

"Could I please wear it to school?" Sara asked.

"Yes," Alice replied, "you can wear it once, if you like, but don't get it dirty".

"I want to wear it tomorrow," said Sara.

"That's fine!" said Alice.

The next day I wore my new Easter coat to school. My teacher, who rarely commented on anyone's clothes, said, "Sara, what a beautiful coat!" "My mother made it," I said. I had never felt so proud!

1948

TWO YEARS AFTER HER DIVORCE WAS FINAL, ALICE REAL-ized that it was time to leave Long Island, where she had lived now for more than 12 years. She wanted to move back to western Massachusetts to be near both her father and her sister Rachel. Alice's dearest friend from high school, Kay Beaver, still lived in that area as well, and living near Kay certainly was an added draw. Alice had left the Springfield area in 1925, after graduating from Central High School. She was then a young girl of 18, full of excitement and hope – a young girl setting off to live and study in the big city of Boston. She would be returning now as a divorced, middle-aged woman with three young daughters to care for and support.

In May of 1948, Alice made an appointment with a real estate agent at Speed & Hegeman in West Springfield – an agency that her sister had recommended. Aunt Florence and Uncle Bill kindly offered to take care of the girls for a few days. Alice made arrangements to stay with her sister, and then drove up to Massachusetts to look for a house. Her thought was that West Springfield, where her sister lived, would be the best place to start house hunting. Springfield, where she had grown up, had become a much bigger city since she was a girl, and many of the young families had moved out to nearby suburbs. Anything located in the area where her father lived, would have been much too expensive for her to even think about. West Springfield was an attractive suburb of Springfield, and, like many of the towns along the Connecticut River, consisted of neighborhoods of varying economic diversity. Most of the least expensive homes were located close to the river, with the house values and quality increasing as one traveled west up the hill and away from the water. The more affluent areas at the top of the hill to the west, where her sister, Rachel, lived, would be not only more expensive, but also less open to having a divorced woman and her family living next door. Alice wisely decided to focus on available houses in the neighborhoods located part way up the hill – in the central part of town.

The next morning, Alice arrived at the realtor's office five minutes early. She was eager to start looking for a new home for her family. The realtor had seven houses lined up to show her, and she looked at each one expectantly. None of them were quite right.

"Don't you have anything else to show me?" she asked hopefully.

"Yes… there is one more . . . but I don't think you'll like it," the realtor replied. "There is a big cemetery just two doors away."

"Well, I'm here. Let's look at it anyway," answered Alice.

Alice liked this grey-shingled house with white shutters as soon as they turned into the driveway. She loved it at first sight. This three bedroom, one bath house had a special charm that appealed to her immediately. She bought it on the spot. It had a large, screened-in porch in the front, a bay window on one side, and a handsome, red brick chimney. In the back of the house was a two-car, detached garage, with room for a vegetable garden behind it. The neighboring house was where the caretaker for the town's Catholic cemetery lived. The cemetery itself consisted of a huge piece of property that extended for at least six blocks to the west. Next door, on the side of the house opposite the cemetery, there was a small, one-story, yellow house lived in by an older couple and their adored only child –a boy. There were no houses at all directly across the street—only an attractive row of evergreens that lined the sidewalk and provided a natural barrier from the properties one street over.

The local elementary school, a two story brick

building that boasted not only a large playground, but also a small baseball diamond, was only a short two blocks away. Within walking distance, as well, was the town reservoir, complete with a sandy beach, where all the neighborhood children gathered to swim and cool off on hot summer days. It was well staffed and monitored, so the older girls would be able to go there on their own.

This charming house that Alice fell in love with, was also situated halfway up the hill on a secondary east-west arterial going through town. Right in front of the house was the spot where every car and every truck going up the hill would shift into a lower gear as they made the ascent. Alice would learn about that very soon after she moved in as the sound of the shifting gears became a familiar part of her day.

In June of 1948, as soon as school was out for the summer, Alice and her three young girls moved into their new home in West Springfield, Massachusetts. Mary Alice was 12, Sara was 10, and Barbara was 7. In the next few years, Alice created a vegetable garden, she and the girls worked on painting or wallpapering all the rooms, and they slowly began to turn this little house into a home.

I believe that either consciously or unconsciously, Mother knew in this house, on this street with the cemetery nearby, and so few neighbors, that the unwanted social stigma that came with being a divorced woman would be minimized. She would not feel the pressure to socialize with the neighboring women, or worry about what they might be thinking about her. She would be free to concentrate on our needs and begin to build a new life for us all. Here she would be perfectly happy with our new neighbors. The dead don't judge!

It was not long after we moved in that Mary Alice and I discovered the cemetery. The cemetery was not fenced in or gated and rarely had any visitors. It was a perfect place for us to play. In fact it often became our playground of choice. The larger tombstones provided wonderful hiding spots for an outdoor game of "Hide and Seek". Mary Alice was endlessly fascinated by the various artistic designs on the stones; and I never tired of reading the birth and death dates. I was also intrigued by the color photos of the deceased on many of the gravestones. I tried to imagine what their lives had been like, how they may have died, and what the world was like in that time long ago.

BEVERLY

THE MOVING MEN WERE UNLOADING THE FURNITURE from the van, but we three sisters had not yet drawn straws to decide who would have her own room and who would have to share a room, when two brown haired kids from the house next door popped in to say "Hi". Beverly Manley was thirteen and her younger brother, Billy, was eleven. Both were delighted to have a family moving in next door. The previous owners of our new house had been older, with children who were grown and no longer lived at home. Beverly and Billy's father was the caretaker for the cemetery that stretched out for several blocks on the other side of the Manley house. No chance for them to find fun playmates over there.

Beverly at thirteen seemed very grown up to me. Billy was closer to my age, but being a boy, and an unusually active one at that, it did not seem as if he would be real friend material. As it turned out, I was mostly right. The next summer, though, Billy figured out an ingenious way to rig up a rope and pulley system between our two houses. We would clip written notes onto the rope with a clothespin, and then send the messages to each other between the houses. That was great fun, but somewhat short lived, as we didn't have a great deal to write about.

The Manley children, especially Beverly, would come over to our house, but I do not remember going to theirs. I believe that Mother soon became aware and sensitive to the fact that their father could be overly strict. Beverly grew to trust Mother and felt safe confiding in her about how difficult her father could be. He would often lose his temper and even strike her sometimes when he got angry. Mother always made time to listen to her and to help her to get her feelings out. She tried to support her with suggestions on how to best deal with the challenges of her home life – things she could not change.

A few years after we moved in, when Beverly was 16 or 17 years old, she came to Mother distraught and in tears. She had missed her last period and was afraid that she might be pregnant. What would she do? Beverly was terrified that her father would beat her when he found out. I wasn't old enough to completely understand, but I knew it was something serious. I was old enough to know that getting pregnant as a teenager when you were not married brought horror, shock, and condemnation. Mother listened to her, and supported her as she faced this unwanted and very difficult situation. She counseled Beverly not to get an abortion. It was a criminal act and was available only through unsafe, underground sources. The only reasonable and safe option for a girl in Beverly's situation was to leave and go to a special home for unwed mothers. This is what Beverly decided to do. I never knew where the home was located, but I do remember that Beverly was away for at least six months. She had to leave her family, her friends, and her school to live with strangers until after the baby was born. Essentially she was banished. At this home she was then counseled to give her baby up for adoption. The thinking at the time was that by giving the baby up for adoption, her pregnancy could effectively be erased from her history, and she could expect to go back to her normal life as if it had never happened. Without her child she could then hope to marry and have other children. Adoption was also viewed as being in the best interests of the child. The child could then be raised in a stable home with a mature married couple without any stigma of illegitimacy.

I don't remember seeing Beverly again, as her family moved away soon after Beverly left for the home for unwed mothers, but I suspect that Mother wrote to her regularly during that time. It would have been like her to continue her support and caring. A young couple with a new baby moved into the Manley house soon after they left.

1948 – Part 2

In September Barbara and I started school at the nearby elementary school just down the street. The school was so close that we could walk there in less than five minutes, so close that we could even come home for lunch if we wanted to. I was in fifth grade and Barbara in second. We both had outstanding teachers – teachers who had taught at the school for many years – and we both soon made friends who lived in the neighborhood. For some reason I immediately assumed a special status. Perhaps it was because of my being the first new girl the class had had since first grade. Maybe it was because of the big green bow I wore in my hair the first day of school, or maybe it was because of my New York accent, but whatever the reason, I created a bit of a stir. At recess time the boys entertained themselves by chasing me around the playground, and then twisting my arm behind my back after they caught me to make me talk. They wanted to hear my New York accent. Obviously none of them had ever traveled out of West Springfield, much less out of Massachusetts. Until then I never realized that people from different areas often have different accents. It took me by surprise, but I must say that I kind of liked the attention.

Mary Alice had a bigger challenge, however. She was the new girl at the large junior high school, which was over a mile away. Her seventh grade class was consisted of graduates from five local elementary schools as well as a parochial school. Every day she faced unfamiliar faces each time the bell rang for a new class period. All the other seventh graders laughed and chatted with friends they had known since kindergarten, but Mary Alice knew no one, and was very, very homesick for her old friends she had left behind on Long Island. Even today she talks sometimes about how hard the move to West Springfield had been for her.

Mother wisely knew that she would have fewer concerns about her children –where they were and what they were doing – if our house and our yard became the place to gather, the place where fun things were happening.

The first summer after we moved in we planned and put on what was to become our annual summer carnival to raise money for local charities. The back yard and back driveway were transformed into a bevy of booths, games and attractions. We had a bean bag toss where the goal was to successfully toss three bean bags through a hole in a piece of plywood. Another booth was "Gone Fishing," where the children holding a fish pole, would drop their line behind a puppet stage, and then someone behind the stage would attach a prize to the line. Throwing rings over milk bottles, and throwing bean bags at tin cans to knock them down, were some of the other challenges set up at booths to win prizes. We all worked for several days ahead of time gathering tables and orange crates, painting signs, finding or buying prizes, and making cookies and lemonade to sell at the carnival. All the neighborhood children came to our carnival. This carnival was to become a yearly event, and was looked forward to both by us, and by all the children who came.

On Halloween we always hosted a neighborhood Halloween party in the basement. The lights were dimmed and the brave party guests were blindfolded. They then had the delight of putting their bare hands into cooked spaghetti that they were told was worms or intestines, and into peeled grapes that they were told were eyeballs. A skeleton hung in the corner and spooky music played on the record player.

Pick-up games of "Capture the Flag" provided hours of fun and excitement for us and for all the neighborhood children. One team claimed the front yard for their territory, and the other team had the back yard. Each side yard was no man's land. There were enough bushes in each team's territory to provide "jails" for any tagged player. It was the perfect house and the perfect yard for "Capture the Flag." We never tired of it.

Mother provided a childhood for us that was so very different from her own. Her growing up years were spent in an adult-centered home with a mother who spent most of her time in bed. She was expected to be as quiet as possible so as not to disturb her ill mother. "Children should be seen, but not heard" was the thinking of the day.

I have often marveled that with no models from her own youth to guide her, Mother somehow created a completely different kind of childhood for my sisters and me. It may have been that times had changed; it may have been that she realized how confining her own childhood had been; it may have been that as a single mother with three children so close together, she was outnumbered; or it may have simply been her own positive and outgoing nature.

The answer probably lies in all of the above, but whatever the reason, my sisters and I were the fortunate beneficiaries. Our childhood had its share of loss, but the overriding message was that the world was a safe and happy place.

Seasons

M OST OF OUR FRIENDS WERE EXPECTED TO HELP WITH the usual household chores – make your bed, wash the dishes, dry the dishes, pick up your room, etc. At our house, however, the word "chores" took on a whole new dimension.

It didn't take Mother long to discover that owning a home as a single woman, with no paid household help, created some very real new challenges. Before the divorce she had had an ironing lady, a cleaning lady, child care help, and a husband who loved to work in the yard. Now she had only herself and three young daughters – not even one son with the potential of a little more muscle to help out.

We moved into our new house on Kings Highway in mid June of 1948, and it wasn't long before it became painfully obvious that someone would have to mow the grass. Hiring someone to mow was out of the question. Mother soon found a used push mower at a reasonable price, had it sharpened, and then proudly brought it home. Mary Alice and

I, ages 11 and 10 at the time were selected to try out the new lawn mower. The yard was not huge, which was good, but it was not perfectly flat either, which was bad. In the front yard one had to push the mower down a slight slope, and then pull it back up, repeating the process all along the front edge of the property. That was the hardest part. Then when the grass catcher filled up, we had to detach it from the mower, carry it all the way to the far end of the property behind the garage, and empty it into the mulch pile.

Autumn followed summer, bringing New England's brilliant fall colors. The leaves on the beautiful deciduous trees turned yellow, orange and red, and the trees in our yard were no exception. The colors were spectacular – signaling it was time to take down the screens and put up the storm windows. Mary Alice and I washed the storm windows, then carefully hung them in place on their brackets. Then the leaves began falling from the trees, piling up in our yard. Very soon the whole yard was covered with brilliant leaves in all their glory. The mowing had ended and the raking began. We two sisters raked the side yard, the front yard, and the driveway. After all the leaves were raked into piles, Mother came outside and supervised as we lit each pile, and watched it burn. She then extinguished the glowing embers. There was usually some time spent jumping into the welcoming piles of leaves before they were burned. The temptation was just too hard to resist, and the fun of jumping in the leaves far outweighed the extra work of raking them back into piles again.

Not long after all the leaves had fallen and the branches were bare, the snowstorms began. Rakes were stowed away, and out came the snow shovels. Snowstorms usually meant a snow day, and a day off from school, but they also meant shoveling. Mary Alice and I shoveled our long driveway and the front walk after each storm. When the shoveling was done, we were free to play in the snow. We would roll enormous snowballs in the front yard, and then carefully carve out the inside to make a snow hut. When the temperature dropped down below freezing, we would sprinkle the hut with water. Soon we had an ice hut that could sometimes last for weeks.

When spring arrived the storm windows came down, and freshly washed screens went up in their place. We helped Mother with many outside chores, but she also needed us to help inside the house as well. There was the usual table setting, dish washing, dish drying, vacuuming, dusting, and kitchen floor washing and waxing; but what I especially remember was the painting. Mother did all the wallpapering, but we were expected to paint all the wood moldings, baseboards and trim. I can still vividly remember every detail of the doorframes and window frames in that special house.

I never felt resentful or put upon by all the chores we were expected to do. Except for the mowing, it all seemed like great fun. We were doing it together, and I enjoyed both the process and the results. When I grew up and had a home of my own, doing all the necessary maintenance activities was not a problem. The only negative feeling that I ever had was a sense of unfairness that our younger sister was rarely required to help either inside the house or outside. Mother's excuse was that since Barbara was three years younger than I was, the chores would have been too hard for her. But then as the years went by, and we all grew older, Mother's excuse became "She is different."

NEIGHBORHOOD HOUSE

THE GIRLS WERE ALL IN BED, AND AS FAR AS SHE KNEW, or at least she hoped, they were finally asleep. At last Alice had a moment to herself to put up her feet, relax, and read the paper. Even though she had grown up just across the Connecticut River in Springfield, she knew very little about West Springfield, the town where she and the girls now lived. Browsing through the local newspaper, the "West Springfield Record," was one way she discovered that she could learn more about the town. She had left Springfield almost a quarter of a century ago as a young woman going off to college in the big city. During that time she had lived in Boston for more than ten years, and then on Long Island with Jim for the eleven years they were married. It felt right to be back in the area where she had grown up, and where her father and sister still lived, but much had changed in the last twenty-five years.

As she leafed through the paper, she came upon an interesting article about the Eastern States Exposition – a large summer fair– in fact one of the biggest fairs in the country. It was going on right now. She promised herself to be sure to take the girls to the fair next summer. She knew they would love all the rides – especially the Ferris wheel, the whip, and the roller coaster. Her eyes then skimmed through the want ads on the last page. One ad immediately caught her eye:

"Sewing teacher needed. Two mornings a week Neighborhood House, Main Street"

"Interesting," thought Alice. "That is something I could do easily, and I certainly know I would enjoy it. Maybe I will go down there tomorrow morning to learn more about the job, the organization, and just what the set up is like for teaching."

The next morning, as soon as the girls had left for school, Alice drove to the Neighborhood House. She turned right by the big White Church with the tall steeple, and headed down the Elm Street hill to the center of town. She took a right onto Main Street, which paralleled the Connecticut River. She wasn't very familiar with this part of town, but she soon located the Neighborhood House, which overlooked the river. Across the water was Springfield, where she had grown up as a girl. As she walked up the sidewalk to the entrance, she noticed that the Boys & Girls Club and the Visiting Nurse Association were located here as well.

"Hello, my name is Alice Hoffman, and I'm here to inquire about the job opening for a sewing teacher that was advertised in the West Springfield Record."

"Yes, you need to talk to Mr. Clark. I will tell him you are here. Please take a seat," said the receptionist.

Alice fidgeted with the folder of credentials she had brought with her, both from The Garland School and from Boston University. She had studied Retailing and Home Economics at The Garland School for two years, and had then transferred to Boston University's School of Education to get a teaching degree. She was certainly qualified for this job – more than qualified.

"Mr. Clark will see you now," said the receptionist.

Alice walked into Mr. Clark's office with some tension and much expectation. Her folder of credentials held tight in her hand. Impressed both by Alice's outgoing personality and sense of style, as well as by her background and experience, Mr. Clark offered her the job on the spot.

"Here is an outline for the course that has been followed in the past. Please feel free to revise it in any way that will work for you. You are the teacher. The class is scheduled to start in three weeks, and so far there are eight people signed up. I would expect a few more. There are 12 sewing machines in the sewing room, so that is the most we can accommodate."

Alice left the office with her head awhirl with thoughts and ideas for the class. She was eager to get home and look over the outline that Mr. Clark had given her. She was a little bit nervous, but mostly excited about the new challenges ahead.

TEACHING

MOTHER WAS A HIGH SCHOOL HOME ECONOMICS teacher for girls in West Springfield, while Mary Alice was in high school. Mother made many women friends there, with whom she socialized at other times. She gave us rides to school both ways, unless there was an after school activity. We were a one-car family. Her only crisis there was when the boyfriend of one of her students barged into class with a knife, and threatened the girl!

Mother used Christian Science prayer to calm them down and diminish her fear. She was successful. We don't remember what happened to him, afterwards.

Because of her own experience of being left alone in her thirties with three daughters to raise by herself, Mother felt very strongly that all women should develop a marketable skill. They should not assume that they would always have a husband to support them.

A high school friend wrote me once, "I think the lady we knew as Mrs. Hoffman took pity on some of the girls her daughters brought home, and tried to help us learn that even FEMALES had choices, and they could make them. Gloria Steinem she wasn't, for I never saw her unforgiving, but she was a beacon of enlightenment before her time. I think she was the only person I told of my interest in Microbiology after having read Paul Dekreif's *Microbe Hunters*. She actually borrowed the book from me."

Mother retired from teaching after marrying her second husband, Johnny, in August of 1959. Mary Alice graduated in 1954, I in 1956 and Barbara in 1958.

1948 – Part 3

A beautiful, clear morning in September – Alice had just said good-bye to the girls as they left the house to walk down the road to school. She was busy washing up the breakfast dishes when the telephone rang.

"Hi, Alice," said a familiar male voice on the other end of the line. It was Jim. She had been expecting his call, but the sound of his voice still made her heart lurch.

"When would be a good time for me to come over?" asked Jim.

"Well, the children get home from school about 3:15 pm. Why don't you come at 3 o'clock, so you will be here when they arrive," suggested Alice.

"I'd like to have a little time to talk to you before the girls get home. Would 2:00 o'clock be okay?" Jim responded.

Alice agreed. She knew that he and Joan had gotten a divorce in May, and that Jim had gotten custody of their 10 month old baby boy, but she didn't know exactly how he had achieved this. With his legal background and expertise, Jim had some how succeeded in proving that Joan was an unfit mother. The requirements needed to be ruled an unfit mother were very strict. One had to be guilty of alcohol or drug addiction, mental illness, sexual abuse, neglect, or abandonment. How he had accomplished this, and gotten custody of the child was hard to fathom, but he had. Jim's sister, Mary Edith, was currently helping him out by taking care of the baby.

Jim rang the doorbell at exactly 2 pm. Being punctual had always been one of his strengths. He gave Alice an unexpected hug as soon as she opened the door. A bit disarmed, Alice showed him into the living room, where they could sit down and talk.

"Did you make these slip covers?" Jim asked, as he sat down. "They are very attractive – especially nice."

"Yes", replied Alice with pride. "I'm glad you like them."

It always pleased her when people praised her work. She never thought of sewing, whether it was dressmaking, tailoring or upholstering, as a chore. To her it was a creative outlet – something she truly enjoyed. She could almost say that it was relaxing, and she often sewed at night at the end of a busy day, after the children were asleep.

"Well, to get to the point," said Jim. "As you undoubtedly must know, Joan and I got divorced in May. I now have custody of Richard. He is a good baby, but I have to admit that caring for an infant can be a challenge at times. Mary Edith has been a wonderful help. I don't know what I would do without her."

"She certainly is the salt of the earth," replied Alice, thinking fondly of her dear friend and sister-in-law, and how much she meant to her. "They don't make them any better."

After moving on to talk about the three girls, and how they were each doing at the start of the new school year, Jim abruptly changed the subject.

"Alice," he said hopefully, "Would you consider marrying me again? I know I have hurt you terribly, and I know I made a foolish mistake, but the truth is that I still love you, and I think that you, the girls and I could all be a family again. I have learned my lesson, and will make it up to you. I promise."

Taken aback, Alice gulped. In spite of everything, she still loved this charming, complicated man. He still had the power to disarm her, and she would undoubtedly always love him in some way, but could she trust him? Did he really want to marry her, or was part of his motivation to have someone to take care of the baby? Her mind raced as she considered the possibility of his proposal. If she agreed to marry him, it would be so simple. They could all be a family again. The girls could have their father back, and she would no longer have to cope with the unwelcome stigma of being a divorced woman. She was certainly flattered – but no, she would not marry him again. She could not marry him again.

"No," she replied with unexpected confidence. She felt a sudden awareness of how much she had grown and changed in the past three years. There was no way to go back to how things were before. The hurt had certainly not gone away, but she was proud of the stronger, wiser woman she had become. She could and would face the future on her own.

"No," she said, "I could never, ever marry you again!"

1948 PART 3, CONTINUED

NO, SHE WOULD NEVER MARRY OUR FATHER AGAIN. SHE would never look back, and she would never regret her decision. Having said this, I suspect that Daddy always remained the love of her life. She could no longer trust him, however, and she was far too smart to put herself in that position again.

But, in spite of her feelings about our father, his relatives were our relatives, and Mother, to her credit, made every effort to support and maintain those very important ties for our sake. Almost every summer through the years when we were growing up, Mother drove from our home in West Springfield, Massachusetts to Grandma and Granddaddy's house in Baltimore, Maryland – a distance of over 300 miles. We visited all our Hoffman relatives – not only our grandparents, but also our two great aunts, Auntie and Aunt Mary as well as our father's sister, Aunt Mimi, her husband, Uncle Freddy, and our cousins, little Mimi and Ricky. We developed very close, warm relationships with all of them, which continue to this day with those that are still living.

Granddaddy Hoffman was a quiet, serious man, revered by his patients, and doted on by his out-going, social wife. Grandma always made sure that his routine was not interrupted, and that his every need was met. I can still picture him sitting all by himself at the head of the dining room table with his back to the kitchen. He always had a soft boiled egg served in a beautiful china egg cup for breakfast every morning.

He was a serious man, but not in anyway uncaring. One of my earliest memories of Granddaddy Hoffman is sitting at his feet while he strummed his guitar, and sang to my sisters and me. Our favorite song, and I suspect his as well, was "Little Sir Echo."

Little Sir Echo, how do you do, hello, hello
Little Sir Echo, I'm feeling blue, hello, hello
Won't you come over and play?
You're a nice little fellow, I know by your voice,
But you're always so far away!

Grandma Hoffman had ongoing household help. Mabel, her maid, was a black woman who came to the house almost every day. One summer when we were visiting, my sisters and I were playing in the street as we often did. Even though our grandparents' house was in the city, very few cars came by during the day. It was quite safe, and actually the only place outside that there was to play. These brick, three-story row houses, with their marble steps in front, and alleys in the back, had essentially no yards. Children played in the street.

One of our favorite jump rope songs was:

Mabel, Mabel, set the table
Don't forget the salt, vinegar
Mustard and pepper.

When the song began the jump rope was rotating at the regular speed, but as soon as the word "pepper" was spoken, the rope was swung twice as fast. One day Grandma, overhearing us, and thinking that we were making fun of Mabel, came running out of the house. She was very, very upset, and scolded us severely. It is the only time I can ever remember her getting angry. Grandma was a warm, outgoing, giving person, and loved us dearly, but the thought that we were making fun of Mabel was more than she could bear.

A number of summers we vacationed at Ocean City, Maryland. The whole Hoffman family, including Grandma and Granddaddy Hoffman, the two great aunts, Auntie and Aunt Mary, as well as Aunt Mimi and her family, and the five of us rented a large house on a short street that ran perpendicular to the ocean and the sound. One of the favorite activities for the older children, when we weren't running on the beach or jumping over waves in the ocean, was catching crabs. We lay on our stomachs on the wharf over the sound dangling fish bait tied to a string, and carefully lowered the bait into the water.

We lay very still with the string in one hand, and a long handled crab net poised over the water in the other hand. As soon as we saw a crab at the bait, we would, in a flash, plunge the net into the water, and scoop it up. When the pail was full of squirming crabs, we carried our catch home to be cooked that night for dinner. It was always fun to catch the crabs, but dreadful to see them face a certain fate as they were dropped into a big pot of boiling water. It wasn't until many years later that I acquired a taste for crab.

An Exciting Day

"**G**IRLS, BE SURE YOU GET ALL YOUR HOMEWORK DONE before dinner. I want to leave for Aunt Rachel and Uncle Albert's house as soon as the dishes are done. The Ed Sullivan show starts at 8 o'clock. Mary Alice, it is your turn to wash," said Alice. "Sara you dry."

As soon as the dishes were done, Alice and the girls hopped into the car, drove past the cemetery, and up Westfield Street to her sister and brother-in-law's house, which was about a mile away.

Sunday night had become our favorite night of the week, ever since Aunt Rachel and Uncle Albert had bought their wonderful, new black and white television set. It was a 17" Zenith console with mahogany exterior. Every Sunday night now, we went to their house to watch the Ed Sullivan show. They had had to move an end table out of the living room, and push a chair to the side to make room for this magical new big box, which was like a miniature movie in your house. As soon as we arrived, the children lined up on the floor in front of the TV, and the grown-ups pulled up chairs behind them waiting for the show to start. In those early days of television, watching TV was always a social event, at least in our family. No one ever watched TV by themselves.

Alice and the girls had always spent quite a bit of time at her sister's house, so this Sunday evenings tradition watch did not seem out of the ordinary. All of their holidays were celebrated together, as well. Christmas, especially, was a big family celebration at Aunt Rachel's and Uncle Al's. As soon as the stockings had been opened, and everyone was dressed, Alice loaded the packages from under the tree into the car, and she and the girls headed to her sister's house for breakfast. After breakfast, and before opening the gifts under the tree, Alice would drive over the river to Springfield to pick up Uncle Raymond. Uncle Raymond was her father's younger brother. He was a bachelor, and now the last of his generation. Alice and Rachel's father, Robert, who was Raymond's older brother, had died just the year before. His sister, Elizabeth, had died in 1905 as a young woman–only 28 years old.

Uncle Raymond, a quiet, gentle man, looked forward to being part of the family celebration on Christmas day. He usually found a chair somewhere in the corner of the room, where he could watch the festivities and be out of the way – this year was no exception.

Shortly after Christmas, Alice was thinking about Uncle Raymond, and wondered to herself whether he wouldn't get some pleasure from having one of these new television sets. It might help entertain him during the long winter evenings. She had some money set aside, and felt that giving Uncle Raymond a TV would be a good way to spend it. The next day she went shopping to see what she could find. She thought she would check the local appliance store, and also see what they had at Sears. To her delight, the appliance store had just the thing–a Magnavox tabletop. The owner of the store, who knew her, gave her a bit off the listed price, which was a big plus.

Feeling elated by her purchase, and with happy thoughts of doing something special for Uncle Raymond, she headed for his house. Alice had always been fond of spouting morals and mottos, especially to her children. One of her favorites was: "When life gets you down, do something for someone QUICK." Now she was doing something for Uncle Raymond, and it felt very, very good.

Uncle Raymond was at home, as she expected, when she arrived at his door with her special surprise in tow. He let her bring the television set into his house, but seemed very nervous and uncertain.

"What will I do with it?" He asked. "Well, why don't you just try it for awhile," replied Alice. "I think you might enjoy some of the shows."

Two days later the phone rang. It was Uncle Raymond on the other end of the line. "Please come take the TV away," he said. "I don't like it, and it makes me very nervous having it in the house." It was just too difficult for him to adjust to something new. He was happy with his radio that he was used to.

"Alright," replied Alice. "I will come get it tomorrow morning as soon as the girls have gone to school."

She picked up the TV the next day and brought it home. When the girls got home from school the new TV was sitting on its stand in the living room.

"Uncle Raymond didn't want it," Alice told them, "so I've decided that we will just keep it. You can watch one show after dinner when your homework is done." We hurried to do our homework as quickly as possible, and then pulled up chairs all in a row to watch "I Love Lucy" with Lucille Ball and Dezi Arnez. It was one of the most exciting days that I can ever remember. We had a TV!

CHRISTIAN SCIENCE

ONCE MARY ALICE AND SARA WERE BOTH IN SCHOOL, Alice realized that it was time to think about taking the girls to Sunday school. She was also feeling a need herself to start going to church again. As a girl growing up in Springfield, Massachusetts, Alice had attended the South Congregational Church on Maple Street, not far from her home. Jim had grown up in the Episcopal Church in Baltimore, Maryland, but had not gone regularly to any church as an adult. Since Alice and Jim had eloped, the topic of church, or church attendance, had not surfaced until now. Alice knew that her father had been interested in Christian Science for some time, and had recently started going regularly to Sunday morning services in Springfield. He had told her that he didn't think Christian Science was the answer, but it was the best thing he had found so far. Since she had always been very close to her dad, she was curious to discover what it was about this church that appealed to him. She was also fascinated to learn that the church had been founded by a woman, Mary Baker Eddy, in 1875, and had become the rage in the late 1880's. Mary Baker Eddy taught that sickness is the result of fear, ignorance, or sin. When the erroneous belief is corrected, the sickness will disappear. She advocated against using medical doctors and encouraged metaphysical work to eliminate fear, ignorance and sin. Since medical science was very primitive at the end of the nineteenth century, in most cases she was right. In most cases one was safer not to go to a doctor.

Alice soon discovered that there was a Christian Science church right in Great Neck not far from where they lived. She would try it out.

"Jim, I just found out that there is a Christian Science church right here in Great Neck. Would you like to go with me to see what it is like?"

"No", replied Jim, "but why don't you go and take the girls."

Alice went with the girls the following Sunday, and she liked what she saw and experienced. She liked the positive emphasis on God as love. The message of a loving god with man made in his image and likeness was very comforting and empowering. She was also intrigued by the fact that the Sunday worship service was the same each week in every Christian Science church all over the world. She liked that you could read the lesson for each week from the Bible and the Science & Health before coming to church on Sunday when it was read to the congregation. The Sunday school was also not like any Alice had seen before. Even the youngest children learned that God is everywhere and that they were made in God's likeness; there is no life, truth, intelligence or substance in matter. Man is spiritual not material. As soon as they were old enough to read they were reading the lesson for each week and discussing it in class. Very little time in Sunday school was spent playing games or coloring.

Two years later when Alice and Jim's marriage began to disintegrate, Alice took advantage of the services of an exceptionally fine Christian Science practitioner at her church. Her counsel and support were vital to Alice as she worked through the emotional stress of the unwanted divorce.

After Alice had moved back to Massachusetts with the girls to be near her father and sister, she found a Christian Science church in Westfield about five miles away. She and the girls went to the church in Westfield every Sunday.

As I look back at this part of Mother's life, I realize that she had made a very wise decision in many ways by taking us to the Christian Science church in Westfield. If she had tried to take us to the local Congregational church that her sister and brother-in-law attended, she would have been viewed by the congregation as a threat to all the couples coming in two-by-two. The Christian Science church in Westfield was not judgmental, had an excellent Sunday School, and an outstanding prac-titioner, Mrs. Gates, whose services Mother used many times through the years.

BARBARA

Y MOTHER WAS A PEOPLE PERSON. SHE LIKED PEOPLE and people liked her. She made friends easily and kept her close friends forever. Her oldest friends were like family to us, and my sisters and I viewed them as relatives. There were Aunt Bunny, Aunt Ruth, and Aunt Kay. People in general were attracted by Mother's vitality and her friendly outgoing manner. She definitely had an innate zest for life. Even though she came from a very privileged background, she liked people for what they were, not for who they were. I observed her when she interacted with store clerks, service people, and gas station attendants. She interacted with them in the same open way she interacted with family and friends. She had worked as a buyer at Filene's and R. H.White's in Boston after she graduated from college, so certainly knew how it felt to be on your feet all day.

Having said that, there is one important and often painful way, in which Mother was a different person. She interacted with my younger sister, Barbara, in a vastly different way than she interacted with my older sister and me. My older sister, Mary Alice, and I were expected to help with all sorts of chores around the house – dishes, vacuuming, lawn mowing, window washing, snow shoveling, painting, etc. Barbara was never expected to do anything, which certainly did not make either Mary Alice or me like her better, to say the least. Mother's only response, when questioned about this, was that Barbara was different.

In retrospect, I believe Mother was quite possibly right. It is very possible that Barbara was born depressed. Barbara never exhibited the same natural energy, curiosity, and outgoingness as a child that Mary Alice and I possessed. One of my early memories of Barbara was when she was about 6 or 7 months old. She was sitting quietly on the floor just looking around. Mary Alice and I – then three and five – decided to build a tower around her with our blocks. Our childhood reasoning was that Barbara would not like being closed in. Not liking it, she would instinctively reach out to knock down the blocks. We were wrong. She never cried. She never reached out to knock down the tower. She just sat there until Mother came looking for her.

Barbara struggled with depression most of her adult life. But, to my knowledge, when she was a child, there was very little awareness of childhood depression, much less that a baby could perhaps be born depressed. Anti-depressants were not available until the early 1960s, and Barbara did not start taking them until the early 1970s. By then she was thirty-one. Mother was right. Barbara was different, but that was not a concept that I could even begin to understand or appreciate as a young girl when it was time to do chores, and not everyone pitched in.

ANYTHING WORTH DOING IS WORTH DOING WELL

MOTHER WAS A PERSON THAT PEOPLE COULD TRUST with their problems – the teenage girl who found herself pregnant, the neighbor whose husband wanted a divorce, the student whose father was abusive. People sensed strength, and intelligence and a caring in Mother. They knew she would listen. They knew they could trust her. They knew she would understand.

"Get it out," she would say. "You can't solve anything by keeping it pent up inside." For me, as a girl growing up with her, I felt she instinctively sensed when I needed to "get it out", and she always found time to listen.

Without being rigid, Mother was in many ways a perfectionist. She was a perfectionist in how she dressed, in the clothes she made, in the meals she cooked, and in the furniture she reupholstered.

"Stand still, don't wiggle," she would say as she

carefully measured and pinned the hems of our skirts. Money may have been tight, but all three of her daughters went to school with flat seams and straight hems.

No one could surpass Mother in the kitchen either. We may not have had steak or lobster, but Mother could make more delicious meals out of a pound of hamburger or a can of tuna fish than anyone I ever knew. She shared her love of food with the girls in her Home Economics class at the high school, and encouraged them to share with her. One year a student from an Italian family demonstrated to the class how to make spaghetti noodles. She mixed the dough, rolled it out, cut the narrow strips, and then carefully hung each strip on a special rack to dry. Mother said they were the best spaghetti noodles she'd ever eaten.

"Anything worth doing is worth doing well," was one of her favorite adages, and she was a living example.

JOHNNY

MY MOTHER MET JOHNNY WHEN SHE WAS TEACHING at West Springfield, during the summer of 1949. Mother was visiting her best friend from childhood, Bunny Whittemore, who had a cottage in Watch Hill, RI. While they were sitting in the cocktail lounge of the Ocean House having drinks, a handsome man, who had been sitting at the bar, passed by on his way to the men's room and smiled at them. On his way back, they smiled at him and something clicked between Mother and Johnny. Thus began their relationship.

Johnny was in the area because he was on leave from a Merchant Marine ship docked at New London, CT. The very next day he was at our house in West Springfield, MA, but stayed at a hotel in Springfield. He remembered rough housing with Mary Alice, who was 12 years-old. Johnny pursued Mother for 10 years, while she tried to make up her mind whether or not to marry him. He was from a much lower social class than she, had no patience with Mother's three girls and was recently divorced, so it was not an easy decision to make. During those years he had a brief marriage on the rebound and had a son, Terry. He wrote love letters to Mother for 10 years, which were found after his death. The box in which they were found was labeled "Treasures" by Mother. Finally, in August of 1959 they eloped. She had said she married Johnny because Jim would always put her down; Johnny didn't. Another motivation for finally marrying Johnny was that Aunt Rachel, her sister, had just lost her husband and Mother didn't want to face what she felt would be inevitable pressure of her moving in with Rachel.

Mary Alice can still remember where she was when Mother called to tell her about marrying Johnny. Mary Alice was in shock and very hurt, but knew her mother had a right to happiness.

Their marriage was not one of the happiest, with Mother frequently putting Johnny down. He silently endured this and years later cared for her, without complaint, for 10 years at home during the progression of Alzheimer's Disease.

Mother spent the last 5 years of her life at Reeds Landing Nursing Home in Springfield, MA, because Johnny was no longer able to lift her when she fell. After 43 years of marriage she passed away on March 27, 2002. Johnny passed away in 2007.

MOTHER'S UNDERLYING PHILOSOPHIES

ANYTHING WORTH DOING IS WORTH DOING WELL

MOTHER WAS NOT WHAT I WOULD CALL A RIGID PERFECtionist, but she always valued doing things correctly. I'll never forget the day I sat beside her in her living room altering a new skirt, so it would fit her better and be more comfortable. Mother was in her early 90's at the time and living with fairly advanced Alzheimer's. Thinking she would not notice, and knowing that she rarely left the house to shop or socialize, I decided to alter the skirt a "quick and dirty" way. While I was busy sewing, Mother jumped out of her chair, came over to me and said, "Stop. You know that is not the right way to face a seam. Take that out and do it over."

WHEN ONE DOOR CLOSES, ANOTHER DOOR OPENS

MOTHER SAID THIS PHRASE FREQUENTLY. I BELIEVE IT WAS one of her basic philosophies. It reflected her positive view of life, and reinforced her belief that living life successfully required being open to and able to embrace change, being able to let go of the past and move into the future.

Made in the USA
Middletown, DE
19 October 2015